The Marriage Course
Leaders' Guide

First published 2000

Published by HTB Publications, Holy Trinity Brompton, Brompton Road, London SW7 1JA

Contents

A: What is involved?

1) The aim of the course

With two out of every five marriages breaking down in the UK, thirty five per cent of them within the first six years, the institution of marriage is under threat today. Some are suggesting that the traditional goal of life-long marriage should be abandoned in favour of an arrangement that makes 'coupling' and 'un-coupling' as easy as possible.

Yet marriage remains of vital importance as the foundation of a stable society. Marriage is the ideal God-given basis of family life, particularly because children learn best what committed, loving relationships are all about through their experience of the commitment between their mother and father.

Many people get married without ever having seen a model of how to build a marriage. They lack the tools that enable them to remain connected. If they stay together, they may exist side by side under the same roof but lose the intimacy between them. They have been embarrassed to seek help or have not known where to find it.

Christians have much to offer. The Bible not only defines what marriage is but also teaches us how to build a marriage over a lifetime. Biblical principles for strong relationships are desperately needed and increasingly sought after in our society.

The aim of *The Marriage Course* is to enable married couples to build a strong and intimate marriage that will last a lifetime. Over eight evenings spent together they find out new things about each other, and new things about themselves. They have the opportunity to talk about issues that have been swept under the carpet in the rush of daily life. They discover what makes their partner feel loved. They have the time to discuss ways they have caused each other pain and discover how to heal the hurt. They recognise the sources of pressure on their relationship. Some learn new skills for communicating and resolving conflict. Others make changes in their lifestyle in order to nurture their marriage. And they grow closer to each other in the process.

Their privacy as a couple is always respected. There is no requirement to disclose anything personal to a third party. But they are expected to talk to each other.

We have been running *The Marriage Course* three times a year at Holy Trinity Brompton since September 1996 with twenty to forty couples on each course. Our experience has shown us again and again that any marriage can be strengthened through doing the course when both husband and wife are prepared to work at their relationship together.

The Marriage Course is designed for others to use whether in a big group or with one or two other couples in their own home. Our hope and prayer is that many courses will be established so that any couple anywhere can find the help and encouragement they need to build their marriage.

2) Who is the course for?

The Marriage Course is for any couple who want to work together at their relationship. Some couples who have attended the course have been married for less than two years, while others for more than thirty.

The course is beneficial and enjoyable for those whose marriage is already strong. It also helps couples who are going through difficulties. They are able to re-open communication in a guided and constructive way. Some couples who are separated or divorced have used the course as a way of trying to get back together.

While the course emphasises and explains the unique nature of marriage, we welcome 'co-habiting' couples if they have been together for some time. Those who have been together for less than two years and are thinking of marriage are encouraged to come on our *Marriage Preparation Course*.

Although the course is based on Christian principles and led by Christians, it is very suitable for those with no Christian faith or church background. We use our own experience in Session 3 to speak of the difference that having

God at the centre makes to a marriage.

Those without a Christian faith are often interested and attracted by what they hear. They are not required to do or say anything that would conflict with their own beliefs. For some such couples it has provided the first contact with the church and we have invited them to follow up *The Marriage Course* by doing an Alpha course together.[1]

3) The design of the course:

The length: The course takes place over seven evenings (or eight including the 'supper parties' – see below). It is best designed with the first four sessions on consecutive weeks and then the last three a fortnight apart. The course is long enough to allow for real change in a relationship. Bad habits can be broken and good habits formed.

'Homework': In between the evenings couples are able to put into practice on their own what they have learnt. Each session includes some 'homework'. This consists of exercises that the guests are encouraged to do at home to help them to continue their conversations in a constructive way.

The supper parties: After the fourth evening, the guests are invited to a supper party hosted by a couple who have previously done the course. Each supper party consists of three or four couples including the hosts. The aim is to have an enjoyable social evening during which the couples can get to know each other. They may discuss the course and what they are getting out of it at the level at which they feel comfortable. The hosts may end the evening with an opportunity to pray for each other, depending on whether those present are Christians.

The supper parties, while not an essential part of the course, have been very enjoyable and helpful for many couples.

The cost: We ask the guests to pay for the cost of supper (including the supper party) when they register for the course. (Bursaries are available.)

---

[1] Alpha is a 15-session practical introduction to the Christian faith designed primarily for non-churchgoers and new Christians

This avoids having to collect money each evening and encourages a greater commitment to do the whole course. It also enables us to give the hosts of the supper parties a contribution towards the cost of the meal. If the cost is thought to be prohibitive or off-putting, a donation for supper could be collected when the guests arrive for each session. For the supper parties, many of our regular hosts are happy to give one at their own expense. An elaborate meal is not required.

Absentees: If a couple are unable to make an evening, we send them a tape of the talk. The money they have paid for supper covers the cost of the tape.

4) The set-up of the room (see Appendix 1)

The environment is crucial to the success of the course. The attention to detail is greatly appreciated by the guests and causes them to feel that their marriage is of high value. The setting up is done before the guests arrive. The atmosphere needs to be warm and welcoming so that the guests feel relaxed and safe.

There is a table for registration near the door with a list of the guests, course manuals and name labels (if the course is large enough to warrant them).

The room is arranged with small tables (enough for one per couple) with tablecloths, napkins and candles. There is sufficient space between the tables for each couple to be able to speak freely without being overheard by others. If the course is being run in a home, couples may use different rooms during the time at the tables to allow sufficient privacy.

Chairs are arranged in pairs at the front of the room where the guests sit for the talks.

There is low lighting (except during the talks) and music is played during supper and when the couples are doing the written exercises and talking together at the tables.

The music system and choice of music needs to allow an even volume and distribution of sound in order to enable each husband and wife to hear one another, but not be heard by another couple. (See Appendix 2 for examples of suitable music.)

There is a display of recommended books on marriage. The simplest system is to have demonstration copies only and order forms from the church bookstall or local Christian bookshop. These can be sent or collected at the following session. (See Appendix 5 for our list of recommended books.)

5) The structure of an evening

The whole evening lasts up to two hours and forty-five minutes but can be shortened by reducing the length of the talks.

Welcome Guests are welcomed warmly as they arrive by at least one of the leaders, and are given a manual. If the course has more than four or five couples, name badges are helpful. A cold non-alcoholic drink is served and the guests are introduced to each other. Many of them are apprehensive on the first evening and the welcome is part of the reassurance they need.

Supper (30 to 40 minutes): This contributes to the effect of the whole evening. Guests have the choice either to sit alone as a couple or to meet other couples around small candle-lit tables over an enjoyable meal. Some tables are laid for two people, others for four or six. They have a main course only as coffee, tea and dessert are served later in the evening.

Many people who have done the course have commented that the supper has made it feel like a special 'evening out' as a couple. If, however, arranging supper proves impossible, the course may be run without it as long as the guests are given something to drink as they arrive and something to eat later in the evening (when they are 'at the tables').

Notices and review (up to 10 minutes): The guests are invited to move to the chairs at the front. We start with a review of the previous session or sessions. On Session 1 each couple tell another couple where they met and what first attracted them to each other, including aspects other than the purely physical! This is the only time we ask them to divulge anything personal to another couple. We stress that it is intended to be fun and that they are not to embarrass their partner. From Session 2, husbands and wives tell their partner what they remember from the previous session(s) that was of particular importance to them.

Talk (*30 to 60 minutes*): The talk starts with some humour and is broken up at intervals with opportunities for husband and wife to talk to one another, sometimes with the aid of an exercise. (These breaks during the talks last between 3 and 10 minutes and the guests remain in the chairs at the front.)

Testimony – optional (*5 minutes*): On some evenings a couple who have done a previous course talk about the difference this particular session has made in their own marriage.

At the tables (*30 to 40 minutes*): The guests move back to the tables. Each couple need a table to themselves at this stage of the evening. There is background music. They do the exercises that have been set, each writing down their thoughts and then discussing together what they have written. Coffee, tea, homemade biscuits, muffins, brownies or fruit are served by the leaders and other helpers as soon as possible to allow the guests to spend the majority of their time together uninterrupted. As the exercises often raise issues that are very personal and may be upsetting, privacy is important.

Concluding remarks and prayer (*10 to 40 minutes*): On some evenings the guests are asked to stay at their tables but at other times they come back to the front for the final section, depending on what is most appropriate. If for some people the evening has brought up painful issues, it is preferable that they stay where they are (unless of course they are in different rooms), rather than feeling exposed by coming back to the front.

The leaders finish the evening with a short closing prayer. From Session 3 the guests are given the opportunity to pray for their husband or wife before they leave.

B: Setting up a course

1) Who should lead it?

The Marriage Course should be led by a Christian couple who have the desire to see marriages strengthened and who feel compassion for those who are struggling. They should have the support of their church leader. They will need to have some experience of leading groups and a willingness to share openly from their own marriage.

It is important that the leaders have first been through all the material themselves, doing the exercises as a couple and discussing the issues raised. They may do the course through the audio tapes with one or two other couples well-known to them. There should be a commitment to continue to build their own marriage and a willingness to be accountable to another couple. There should be no major unresolved issues between them.

Leading *The Marriage Course* will often strengthen a couple's own marriage through reminding them of important principles and through their working together, but it is not uncommon for the leaders' own relationship to come under pressure during the course. It is therefore important that they have others who are praying for them and to whom they can turn for encouragement and support.

The leaders will also need other mature Christian couples to support them in providing specific help for guests who request it. These couples should also have done *The Marriage Course* and may give a testimony on the current course. This will help the guests to get to know them.

In addition the leaders should know where to refer couples for professional help if the issues that arise are beyond their own experience or the capabilities of their team. This might be the case where a guest needs counselling as a result of childhood abuse or where there are complex sexual issues. (The bibliography in *The Marriage Book* gives some suggestions.)

2) Establishing a 'taskforce'

This team supports all aspects of the course including:

- setting up the room
- preparing supper
- serving supper
- welcoming guests as they arrive
- clearing and washing up
- resetting the tables after supper
- re-lighting the candles when needed
- helping to serve coffee and tea
- turning the music on and off

The number of helpers required on the taskforce will depend on the size of the course. Even with a course of two or three couples the leaders will benefit from having others who can help them so that they are free to give their full attention to the guests.

On the second and subsequent courses, guests from previous courses are invited to help on one or more evenings. Many couples are glad of the opportunity to give something back as well as to hear a particular talk again.

3) Resources required

- *The Marriage Course Leaders' Guide*
- A manual for each of the guests (two per couple)
- A set of audio tapes of the course
- *The Marriage Book* by Nicky and Sila Lee (HTB publications, 2000)
- Music (suitable music suggested in Appendix 2)

- Tables and chairs

- Tablecloths, candles, candleholders and napkins

- Supper, coffee and tea-making facilities

- An overhead projector ('OHP' – not essential, but helpful for displaying enlarged diagrams from the manual)

- Lectern or other stand for speakers' notes

4) Preparing to lead an evening

If the group is small enough, the course can be done with audio tapes. The leaders will need to know for how long to stop the tape for each exercise (see the timetable for each evening).

If you are giving the talks yourselves, start your preparation at least a week before. (Speakers' notes of the talks are to be made available on CD-ROM. These may be adapted as you include illustrations from your own marriage, and may be shortened.)

We have found it helpful to prepare the evening together.

- Talk through the plan for the session and any concerns you may have

- Start your preparation with a prayer

- Listen to the tape of the particular session and read the relevant section of *The Marriage Book*

- Decide who will do each section of the talks

- Work out what you are going to share from your own experience

- Adjust the speakers' notes (if using the CD-Rom) adding illustrations from your own marriage

- Go through this with each other to make sure that you are agreed about what you will include. Do not include anything that would offend, belittle or otherwise upset your partner

- Make sure that you feel comfortable with the material and are familiar with the exercises

If another couple who have already done *The Marriage Course* are giving a testimony, it is worth preparing them. The main aim of the testimony is to illustrate the benefits of the session from the couple's own experience. The testimony should be about five minutes; interviewing them enables the leader to guide what they say and to limit the length if necessary. Both husband and wife should speak. Find out beforehand what difference the session made to their marriage and ask questions that will keep the testimony personal and helpful to the guests. (Natural humour is a great asset.) Some helpful questions are:

- How would you describe your marriage when you started the course?

- What happened on this session?

- What difference has it made to your relationship since then?

5) Feedback

A questionnaire has been developed to be distributed on the last evening (see Appendix 4). This serves as a review of the course for the guests and provides helpful feedback for the leaders to know how to make the course more effective the next time.

6) How to promote the course

We need to remove the stigma involved in doing a marriage course. It is not an admission of failure nor an indication that a couple's marriage is in trouble. In the same way that many people today do courses to enhance their skills in management, computing or mechanics, this is a course to enhance their marriage.

You may run the course within your church or within the local community. Whatever the setting, the message is the same: '*The Marriage Course* is for anyone who is married to help them to get the most out of their marriage. It is based on Christian principles but is very suitable for non-churchgoers. It gives couples skills to grow together and to deepen their intimacy with each other. And it is enjoyable too!'

Make clear that couples will not be required to divulge anything about their own marriage to anybody else, but they will be encouraged to talk to each other.

There is a great advantage in running two or three courses a year as most guests come on the recommendation of others who have already done it.

After the first course, a testimony at a Sunday service by a couple who have done the course, enjoyed it and benefited from it, will encourage others to come. It is important that the testimonies are kept personal by asking such questions as:

- Why did you decide to do *The Marriage Course*?

- What did you get out of the course?

- What difference has it made to your marriage?

Create a plan for publicising your course. Allow at least eight weeks before the course begins. Print invitations (see the example in Appendix 3) and encourage people to give these to their friends. Ask if an announcement may be made in your church and possibly in other churches nearby. Use publicity through a local paper, schools or doctors' surgeries if you are ready to reach a wider audience.

7) Registering a course

If you are planning to run a *Marriage Course* please let us know at Holy Trinity Brompton, Brompton Road, London SW7 1JA or via our website www.htb.org.uk. This will enable us to support you in the future and direct any enquiring couples who live in your area to your course if appropriate.

C: An overview and timetable for each evening

Session 1 – Building Strong Foundations

1) Overview:

Closeness in marriage must be nurtured. It is essential we find time together and understand each other's needs. This session causes couples to look at their lifestyle and its effect upon their marriage, and to learn more about each other's needs and desires.

2) Resources: *The Marriage Book* – Section 1

The Marriage Course – Tape 1

3) Checklist: A manual for each guest

Music – during supper

– at the tables

– at the end

Name labels

Overhead projector ('OHP'– optional)

OHP slides of the 'marriage wheel' and exercises 1 and 2 enlarged (Session 1 only)

Cold drink

Supper

Tea, coffee and dessert

Tables, tablecloths and chairs

Napkins, candles and candleholders

Spare pens

Book table

Speakers' stand

Jug of water, glass and tray for visual aid (Session 1 only)

Guest attendance list

4) Timetable:

Times:

From 6.30pm Be ready! (Guests often arrive early on the first evening.) Welcome and offer a cold drink

7.00 **Supper**

7.35 Invite guests to the chairs at the front

7.40 **Notices**

- 'Please write your name on your manual'

- Mention the date of the supper parties and explain the purpose of them. (Invitations will be given out on Session 3)

- 'If you get stuck at any point on the course please tell us. We or another couple would be delighted to see you privately'

- 'Let us know if you can't come for one of the evenings and we will give/send you the tape'

- 'Relax! You will not be required to disclose anything private about your relationship after the next exercise'

- 'For a bit of fun, tell one other couple where you met and what first attracted you to each other (including aspects other than the purely physical!)'

7.50	**Talk** – *What is marriage?*
8.15	**Testimony** – (if available)
8.20	**Exercise** – *Taking stock of your marriage* (at the tables)
8.45	Give a five minute warning before calling guests back to the front
8.50	**Talk** – *Making time for each other*
9.10	**Talk** – *Understanding one another*
9.20	**Exercise** – *Knowing me, knowing you*
	(stay in chairs at the front)
9.30	**Survey**

- 'How many chose the same requests as their husband or wife?'

- 'How many guessed correctly what their husband or wife had written?'

9.35 **Conclusion**

- Explain and encourage the 'homework'

- End with a short prayer

Session 2 – The Art of Communication

1) Overview:

Listening is a skill that can and must be learned for a strong marriage. Couples practise communicating their feelings and listening effectively to each other.

2) Resources: *The Marriage Book* – Section 2

The Marriage Course – Tape 2

3) Checklist: As for Session 1

Spare guest manuals

An issue that one of you has thought of to use for the leaders' demonstration of *effective listening*

Two chairs for the leaders' demonstration

A handkerchief or napkin for the leaders' demonstration

4) Timetable:

From 6.45pm   Welcome guests with a drink

7.00   **Supper**

7.35   Invite guests to the chairs at the front

7.40   **Notices**

- 'Please bring your manuals for each session – there are spare ones for any who have forgotten theirs'

- 'If you get stuck on the course at any point please let us know'

Review

- 'Tell your husband or wife what you remember from the last session'

7.45
- Ask the whole group what they remember from Session 1

- Remind of the importance of 'Marriage Time'

- Remind of the importance of understanding each other's desires: 'We can't assume our desires are the same. I can't assume I know my partner's desires. I can't assume they instinctively know mine'

7.50   **Talk** – *Introduction – Effective communication – The importance of listening*

8.05   **Exercise** – *The power of listening*
(stay in chairs at the front)

8.10   **Feedback** – Collect short answers to the exercise from the group as a whole

8.12   **Talk** – *Hindrances to listening*

8.30   **Exercise** – *A childhood memory*
(stay in chairs at the front)

8.35   **Talk** – *Principles for effective listening*

8.45   **Leaders' demonstration of effective listening**
- Before the evening, one of you needs to have thought of an issue that you have not previously discussed. (Do not choose an issue that would be deeply hurtful or embarrassing for your husband or wife.)

- This person holds the handkerchief to remind both of you whose issue it is

- Using the five principles for effective listening, demonstrate in front of the whole group what effective listening looks like and sounds like (as on the tape)

8.55   **Exercise** – *Effective listening* (at the tables)

9.30   **Conclusion** (stay at the tables)

- Ask what it felt like to be listened to

- Ask if it was hard not to interrupt or give advice

- End with a short prayer eg 'Lord, thank you that you are always listening to us. Help us to be good at listening to each other that we may grow in our understanding and support of one another. Amen'

Session 3 – Resolving Conflict

1) Overview:

Problems can strengthen a marriage when a couple tackle them together. Their togetherness is helped by expressing their appreciation of each other, recognising their differences of temperament, learning to negotiate disagreements and praying together.

2) Resources: *The Marriage Book* – Section 4

The Marriage Course – Tape 3

3) Checklist: As for Session 1

Spare guest manuals

OHP slide of Exercise 2 – *Recognising our differences* enlarged from the manual (optional)

Invitations to supper parties

3) Timetable:

From 6.45pm Welcome guests with a drink

7.00 Supper

7.35 Invite guests to the chairs at the front

7.40 Notices

- Ask the guests to reply to the supper party invitations by contacting their hosts

Review

- 'Tell your husband or wife one occasion over this last week when they met one of your requests from Session 1, Exercise 2 – *Knowing me, knowing you* (page 13 of the manual)'

7.45 **Talk** – *Introduction – Expressing our appreciation of each other*

8.00 **Exercise 1** – *Showing appreciation* (stay in chairs at the front)

8.10 **Talk** – *Recognising our differences*

8.20 **Exercise 2** – *Recognise your differences* (stay in chairs at the front)

8.30 **Talk** – *Negotiating areas of conflict*

8.45 **Testimony** – (if appropriate)

8.50 **Exercise 3** – *Changing our behaviour* (at the tables)

9.15 Give a five minute warning before starting the next section of the talk

9.20 **Conclusion** – *Learning to pray together* (guests stay at the tables)

9.40 Give couples the option either to discuss what they have heard or to ask their husband or wife one thing they can pray for and then to pray for each other aloud or silently

9.45 Close with a short prayer

Session 4 – The Power of Forgiveness

1) Overview:

Apology and forgiveness are essential to restore trust and intimacy when we have hurt each other. This session helps couples to put this into practice for past and present hurts.

2) Resources: *The Marriage Book* – Section 5

The Marriage Course – Tape 4

3) Checklist: As for Session 1

Spare guest manuals

OHP slide of the house of cards enlarged from the manual (optional)

4) Timetable:

From 6.45pm   Welcome guests with a drink

7.00   **Supper**

7.35   Invite guests to the chairs at the front

7.40   **Notices**

- Encourage guests to reply to their supper party invitation if they have not done so

Review

- Review of Session 3 – ask couples to talk about whether they have had a more positive atmosphere in their home over the past week by working through problems together rather than attacking or criticising each other

7.50   **Talk** – *How can intimacy be lost?*

               – *How can intimacy be restored?*

               1)   Identify hurt

               2)   Apologise

8.20   **Testimony** – (if appropriate)

8.25   **Explain exercise** – and pray a short prayer for God's help

8.30   **Exercise** – *Identifying unresolved hurt* (at the tables)

9.05   Give a five minute warning before doing the conclusion

9.10   **Conclusion** – *How can intimacy be restored?* (cont.)

               3)   Forgiveness

               4)   Start again together

9.40   Encourage couples to do the homework. Give an opportunity for couples to pray for their partner

9.45   Close the evening with a short prayer

Session 5 – Parents and In-laws

1) Overview:

Couples are helped to recognise how their family background affects the way they relate to each other. They also consider how to build a good and healthy relationship with their parents, in-laws and wider family now.

Leaders need to be aware that this session can bring up unresolved hurt from the past which may take longer to resolve than the course allows.

2) Resources: *The Marriage Book* – Section 6

The Marriage Course – Tape 5

3) Checklist: As for Session 1

Spare guest manuals

Bag of 10 small coins on each table

OHP slides of the four stages of family development and of the exercise *Reflect on your upbringing* (optional)

4) Timetable:

From 6.45pm Welcome guests with a drink

7.00 **Supper**

7.35 Invite guests to the chairs at the front

7.40 **Notices**

- Encourage couples to ask for help if they get stuck over an issue that the course has raised, particularly as a result of this evening

Review

- 'Looking at this week's reminder section in the manual, tell your partner either, "You're good at....," or, "I need to ......," but not, "You need to...."'

7.50   **Talk** – *Introduction – Growing up – Relating well to parents*

8.10   Couples to talk about most relevant section for them (stay in chairs at the front)

8.15   **Talk** – *Letting go and moving on*

8.35   **Testimony** – (if appropriate)

8.40   **Explain exercise** – *Reflect on your upbringing* (demonstrating how to use the coins with the OHP, if available)

8.45   **Exercise** – *Reflect on your upbringing* (at the tables)

9.15   **Conclusion** – *Healing childhood pain*

9.35   To help those who still carry pain from their childhood, lead the guests in a prayer expressing forgiveness towards parents or others. Then ask God to heal the hurt (as in *The Marriage Book* page 221)

9.40   Give the guests the opportunity to pray for their husband or wife. Offer to talk and/or pray with any of the guests who would like to. They might want to arrange to do this at another time during the week

Session 6 – Good Sex

1) Overview:

Sexual intimacy needs to be worked at and developed. Couples are able to communicate about their expectations and disappointments and to recognise where they need to make changes.

Leaders who give their own talks need to be able to talk about this subject without embarrasment and with some gentle humour. This helps the guests to address this area of their marriage with openness.

2) Resources: *The Marriage Book* – Section 7

The Marriage Course – Tape 6

3) Checklist: As for Session 1

Spare guest manuals

4) Timetable:

From 6.45pm	Welcome guests with a drink
7.00	**Supper**
7.35	Invite guests to the chairs at the front
7.40	**Review**
	• Talk as a couple about: 'What was most important for you from the last session on parents and in-laws?'
7.45	**Talk** – *How we view sex*
8.00	**Talk** – *Six qualities of great lovers*
	1) The importance of communication

	2) The importance of tenderness
8.20	Short break
8.23	**Talk** – *Six qualities of great lovers* (continued)
	3) The importance of responsiveness
	4) The importance of romance
8.33	Short break
8.36	**Talk** – *Six qualities of great lovers* (continued)
	5) The importance of anticipation
	6) The importance of variety
8.45	**Exercise** – *Talking about sex* (at the tables)
9.15	**Conclusion** – *Protecting our marriage* (stay at the tables)
9.35	Close with a short prayer. Give the guests an opportunity to pray for their partner and then leave in their own time. Offer to talk and/or pray with any of the guests before they leave

Session 7 – Love in Action

1) Overview:

There are five ways of expressing love – through words, time, touch, presents and actions. Couples discover which expression of love is most important for their partner and how to show love to them consistently in this way.

2) Resources: *The Marriage Book* – Section 3

The Marriage Course – Tape 7

The Five Love Languages by Gary Chapman (Northfield 1995)

3) Checklist: Spare guest manuals

Questionnaire (one per guest)

Invitations to the next *Marriage Course*

Presents for the 'taskforce'

4) Timetable:

From 6.45pm   Welcome guests with a drink.

7.00   **Supper**

7.35   Invite guests to the chairs at the front.

7.40   **Review**

- Ask the guests to fill in the questionnaire. They will complete the final section at the end of the evening

7.50   **Notices**

• Thank the taskforce and give small presents to those who have helped each week, especially if they are unmarried

• Encourage the guests to take invitations to the next *Marriage Course* to give to others

• Encourage the guests to seek further help if the course has revealed areas of ongoing difficulties. (Having on the book table the card of a counsellor, who specialises in sex therapy, can help a guest or a couple who may be embarrassed to talk to the leaders.)

7.55   **Talk** – *The five expressions of love*
(Give a three minute break after number 3, 'Physical affection'.)

8.45   **Testimony** – (if appropriate)

8.50   **Exercise** – *Discover your partner's and your own 'love language(s)'* (at the tables)

9.20   Ask guests to complete the questionnaires (stay at the tables)

9.25   **Conclusion**

• Tell the guests how much you have enjoyed doing the course (if you have!)

• Encourage them to finish any homework they have not managed during the course

• Give the guests the opportunity to pray for their partner

• Finish the course with a prayer

• Collect questionnaires before the guests leave

Appendix 1: Suggested room set-up

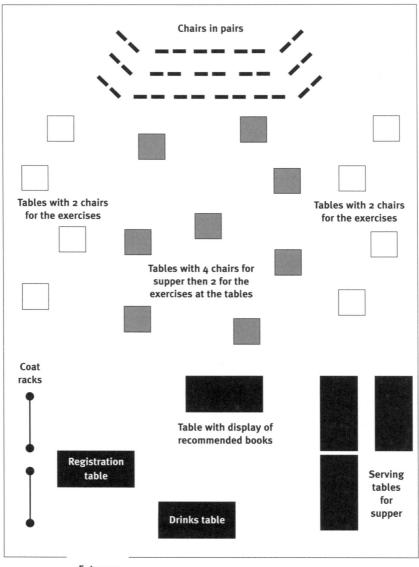

Chairs in pairs

Tables with 2 chairs
for the exercises

Tables with 2 chairs
for the exercises

Tables with 4 chairs for
supper then 2 for the
exercises at the tables

Coat
racks

Table with display of
recommended books

Registration
table

Serving
tables
for
supper

Drinks table

Entrance

Appendix 2: Examples of suitable music

The background music played while the couples are at the tables needs to be of an even volume. Otherwise, during the quieter sections, the couples will be overheard and, during the louder sections, they won't be able to hear their partner. We use a variety of classical and contemporary music, aiming to match the mood of the music to the nature of the exercise.

At the end of the evening, the music needs to be reasonably quiet as, from Session 3, the guests are given the opportunity to pray for their husband or wife.

The following list is for example only. The type of music used should be adjusted to match the musical taste of the guests.

Session 1

Supper   Mozart – 'Symphonie Concertanti' and 'Rondo'

At the tables   C P E Bach – 'Flute Concertos'

End   Andy Piercy & Dave Clifton – 'Psalms, hymns & spiritual songs'

Session 2

Supper   Enya – 'Shepherd Moons'

At the tables   Albinoni – '12 Concertos, op. 9'

End   Albinoni – '12 Concertos, op. 9'

Session 3

Supper   Mozart – 'Horn Concertos'

| At the tables | The choir of Trinity College Cambridge – 'Vocé' |
| End | The choir of Trinity College Cambridge – 'Vocé' |

Session 4

Supper	'For the one I love – 12 instrumental songs of love' – Kingsway Music
At the tables	Maire Brennan – 'Perfect Time'
End	Solo Christian artist (e.g. Martyn Joseph – 'Being Here' – quieter tracks)

Session 5

Supper	Mozart – 'Flute Concertos No. 1 & 2; Flute/Harp Concerto'
At the tables	J S Bach – 'Double Concertos'
End	Iona – 'Open Sky' (quieter tracks)

Session 6

Supper	The Covenant – 'My Utmost for His Highest'
At the tables	J S and C P E Bach – 'Oboe Concertos'
End	Solo Christian artist (quieter tracks)

Session 7

Supper	Keith Jarrett – 'The Melody At Night, With You'
At the tables	J S Bach – 'Violin Concertos'
End	Iona – 'Open Sky' (quieter tracks)

Appendix 3: The Marriage Course Invitation

We would like to invite you to:

THE MARRIAGE COURSE

led by Nicky and Sila Lee

at 7.00 p.m. for supper
at Holy Trinity Brompton

on Monday 8, 15, 22, 29 May
5, 12, 26 June
10 July

The Marriage Course will give practical help to enable married couples to:

communicate more effectively and deeply
learn how to handle and resolve conflict
develop trust
develop friendship and romance
grow in emotional, physical and spiritual intimacy

COST: £60 (per couple, which includes
supper and materials)
Bursaries available

RSVP: Nicky and Sila Lee
Holy Trinity Brompton
Brompton Road
London SW7 1JA
020 7590 8268

Appendix 4: The Marriage Course Questionnaire (A4 size – double-sided)

The Marriage Course

This questionnaire is a great help in developing the course and we would be grateful if you would answer as thoroughly as you can. Your answers will remain confidential:

Name *(or anonymous if preferred):*   How long married?

1. How did you find out about *The Marriage Course?*

2. What issues, if any, did you have in your marriage before you started the course?

3. In what ways, if any, has the course helped and improved your marriage?

4. What were the most important things you learnt on the course?

5. What did you enjoy most about the course?

6. What, if anything, did you find difficult?

7. Did you manage to do the homework?

If so, in what ways was it useful?

8. Have you managed to build 'marriage time' into your weekly routine during the course?

If so, how useful has it been?

Do you intend to keep this up in the future?

9. How could we improve the course?

Summer 2000

Date	Title	On a scale of 1 – 5, please circle how helpful each evening has been 1– not helpful 5 – extremely helpful	Please explain why it was helpful or not helpful:
8th May	'Building strong foundations'	1 2 3 4 5	
15th May	'The art of communication'	1 2 3 4 5	
22nd May	'Resolving conflict'	1 2 3 4 5	
29th May	'The power of forgiveness'	1 2 3 4 5	
12th June	'Parents and in-laws'	1 2 3 4 5	
26th June	'Good sex'	1 2 3 4 5	
10th July	'Love in action'	1 2 3 4 5	
5th June	Supper Party	1 2 3 4 5	

Appendix 5: Recommended books

Gary Chapman, *The Five Love Languages* (Northfield Publishing 1995)

Gary Chapman, *The Other Side of Love – Handling Anger in a Godly Way* (Moody Press 1999)

Gary Chapman, *Hope for the Separated* (Moody Press 1982)

Nicky Gumbel, *30 Days* (HTB Publications 1999)

Nicky Gumbel, *Questions of Life* (Kingsway 1993)

Selwyn Hughes, *Marriage as God Intended* (Kingsway 1983)

Nicky and Sila Lee, *The Marriage Book* (HTB Publications 2000)

Mike Mason, *The Mystery of Marriage* (Triangle 1997)

Rob Parsons, *Loving Against The Odds* (Hodder & Stoughton 1994)

Rob Parsons, *The Sixty Minute Marriage* (Hodder & Stoughton 1997)

Mary Pytches, *Yesterday's Child* (Hodder & Stoughton 1990)

Ed and Gaye Wheat, *Intended for Pleasure* (Scripture Union 1979)

Ed and Gaye Wheat, *Love Life for Every Married Couple* (Marshall Pickering 1984)

Philip Yancey, *What's So Amazing About Grace?* (Zondervan Publishing House 1997)

Daily Light (Tyndale Press 1999)